The Prospects and Perils of Catholic-Muslim Dialogue

Robert R. Reilly

Faith & Reason Institute
The Westminster Institute
Isaac Publishing

The Prospects and Perils of Catholic-Muslim Dialogue by Robert R. Reilly
Copyright © 2013 Faith & Reason Institute and The Westminster Institute

Published in the United States by
Isaac Publishing
6729 Curran Street
McLean, Virginia 22101

For more information about obtaining additional copies of this Westminster Institute
publication, please visit the Institute's website at www.westminster-institute.org,
call 1-703-288-2885, or email info@westminster-institute.org.

ISBN: 978-0-9892905-6-2

Book design by Lee Lewis Walsh, Words Plus Design

Printed in the United States of America

The Prospects and Perils of Catholic-Muslim Dialogue

"Upon Muslims, too, the Church looks with this esteem." – *Nostra Aetate*

"And nearest among them in love to the believers thou wilt find those who say: 'we are Christians.'" – Q 5.85

From the Christian perspective, it seems that there is little dispute over the necessity of dialogue between the Catholic Church and Islam, the world's two largest religious denominations. In Cologne on August 20, 2006, Benedict XVI said, "Interreligious and intercultural dialogue between Christians and Muslims cannot be reduced to an optional extra. It is, in fact, a vital necessity, on which in large measure our future depends." At the Vatican on March 22, 2013, his successor, Francis I, said, "It is not possible to establish true links with God, while ignoring other people. Hence it is important to intensify dialogue among the various religions, and I am thinking particularly of dialogue with Islam."

This study will begin with a look at 20th-century and more recent Vatican and papal pronouncements on the subject of dialogue with Muslims. What are the reasons for it? What can it hope to achieve? And what reservations have been expressed regarding its limitations? This study will then consider the potential problems for dialogue in the context of the historical background of the predominant Islamic theological school, as it has developed from the 9th century till today. This is extremely important, because this school, Ash'arism, defined reality for a large part of the Muslim world, and still does. Next, with this perspective in mind, we will analyze the contemporary Muslim responses to Benedict's statements on Islam, particularly from the *Regensburg Lecture*. The paper will conclude with a critical assessment of the prospects for dialogue, with a special focus on how dialogue has been conducted in the United States by the three regional conferences of the National Catholic Conference of Bishops.

In *Guidelines for Dialogue between Christians and Muslims*, from the Pontifical Council for Interreligious Dialogue, Fr. Maurice Borrmans, one of the pioneers of dialogue, wrote that "...Christians and Muslims seem now to have entered a time of respect and understanding in which Christians, for their part, try to appreciate Muslims on the basis of the best in the latter's religious experience." This perspective is essential for any appreciation of Islam. If approached in this manner, a great deal in the Muslim way of life can be grasped with sympathetic understanding.

Consider, for instance, this entreaty: "O God, I ask of you a perfect faith, a sincere assurance, a reverent heart, a remembering tongue, a good conduct of commendation, and a true repentance, repentance before death, rest at death, and forgiveness and mercy after death, clemency at the reckoning, victory in paradise, and escape from the fire, by your mercy, o mighty One, Forgiver. Lord, increase me in knowledge and join me to the good."

Certainly, not much, if anything, would need to be changed in this prayer for a Christian to say it. Yet it is what Muslims recite at the seventh circumambulation of the *ka'ba* during the *haj* in Mecca. The spiritual impulses and hopes that this prayer expresses make more or less immediately apparent to Christians what they may share in common with Muslims in the best of their religious experience. One must begin, therefore, in any appraisal of the prospects for dialogue with an understanding that Muslims sincerely seek the will of Allah.

What the Catholic Church Says

Perhaps the most compelling impetus for dialogue is charity. Several recent popes, including Benedict XVI, have quoted Gregory VII's missive in 1076 to Al-Nasir, the Muslim Ruler of Bijaya (present day Algeria): "Almighty God, who wishes that all should be saved and none lost, approves nothing in so much as that after loving Him one should love his fellow man, and that one should not do to others, what one does not want done to oneself. You and we owe this charity to ourselves especially because we believe in and confess one God, admittedly, in a different way, and daily praise and venerate him, the creator of the world and ruler of this world."

Needless to say, charity has not been the principal feature of Catholic-Muslim relations over 1,400 years. However, efforts for dialogue began in earnest some 50 years ago, inspired by two church documents. They were preceded in August, 1964, by Pope Paul VI's encyclical letter on the church, *Ecclesiam suam*, in which he commended "adorers of God according to the conception of monotheism, the Muslim religion especially, [as] deserving of our admiration for all that is true and good in their worship of God." Then, four months later, the *Dogmatic Constitution on the Church* announced that the "plan of salvation also includes those who acknowledge the Creator. In the first place amongst these there are the Mohammedans, who, professing to hold the faith of Abraham, along with us adore the one and merciful God, who on the last day will judge mankind" (*Lumen Gentium* 16).

The second and most extended Vatican II reference to Islam comes in the *Declaration on the Relation of the Church to Non-Christian Religions, Nostra Aetate* (Second Vatican Council, October 28, 1965), which makes clear what "is true and good in their worship of God":

> The Church regards with esteem also the Moslems. They adore the one God, living and subsisting in Himself; merciful and all-powerful, the Creator of heaven and earth, who has spoken to men; they take pains to submit wholeheartedly to even His inscrutable decrees, just as Abraham, with whom the faith of Islam takes pleasure in linking itself, submitted to God. Though they do not acknowledge Jesus as God, they revere Him as a prophet. They also honor Mary, His virgin Mother; at times they even call on her with devotion. In addition, they await the day of judgment when God will render their deserts to all those who have been raised up from the dead. Finally, they value the moral life and worship God especially through prayer, almsgiving and fasting.
>
> Since in the course of centuries not a few quarrels and hostilities have arisen between Christians and Moslems, this sacred synod urges all to forget the past and to work sincerely for mutual understanding and to preserve as well as to promote together for the benefit of all mankind social justice and moral welfare, as well as peace and freedom.

These are, no doubt, ambitious goals. They have been, more or less, repeated since then. John Paul II expressed the wish that interreligious dialogue would lead to many forms of cooperation, reflecting the mutual "obligations to the common good, to justice and to solidarity." Reflecting upon his trip to Turkey in 2006, Benedict XVI said, "Christians and Muslims should collaborate together on issues like justice, peace and life."

However, do the Church and Islam share similar conceptions as to what constitutes the common good and justice that could undergird such cooperation? Do they even have the same epistemologies? Is there a general acknowledgment, on both sides, that Catholics and Muslims should be "in partnership for the good of the human family"?

The urge to answer in the positive is so great as to make these questions seem almost rhetorical. However, they are not. They require careful examination in order not to lose sight of essential principles. In an address to organizations for interreligious dialogue, Benedict XVI cautioned that "truth makes consensus possible, and keeps public debate rational, honest and accountable, and opens the gateway to peace." If dialogue is a necessity impelled by charity, it nevertheless cannot exclude the obligation to truth. With this in mind, one must wonder over the prospects for its success. How is such dialogue to be conducted and with whom? What are its grounds? Of course, there are provisional answers to these questions, since some kind of dialogue has been officially conducted since the time of Paul VI.

Reservations Concerning Dialogue

As frequent as papal exhortations to dialogue have been, they are almost always accompanied by the cautionary requirement "to defend freedom of religion, which is the right of every human being" (John Paul II's address to Christians and others in Bangladesh, November 19, 1986). In addressing Muslims on numerous occasions, Benedict XVI repeatedly emphasized "the dignity of the human person and of the rights ensuing from that dignity" (Regensburg, September 25, 2006), and "the sacred character and dignity of the person" (Turkey, November 28, 2006). In Turkey, Benedict also said that "freedom of religion, institutionally guaranteed and effectively respected in practice, both for individuals and communities, constitutes for all believers the necessary condition for their loyal contribution to the building up of society..." In Jordan, on May 9, 2009, Benedict XVI spoke of "our common human dignity, which gives rise to universal human rights."

To Muslims in Berlin, on September 23, 2011, Benedict stated, "This mutual respect grows only on the basis of agreement on certain inalienable values that are proper to human nature, in particular, the inviolable dignity of every single person as created by God." Benedict believed there could "be fruitful collaboration between Christians and Muslims," but only if common ground can be found in recognition of "inalienable rights that are proper to human nature and precede every positive formulation." As the Second Vatican Council said, religious freedom "has its foundation in the very dignity of the human person, as this dignity is known through the revealed word of God and by reason itself" (*Dignitatis humanae*, No. 10). It is particularly the latter source of this knowledge – "reason itself" – that Benedict XVI emphasized in his colloquies with Muslims, as reason is what makes this knowledge universally available.

These statements might seem so standard as to be harmless, almost boilerplate, but they are, in fact, very pointed and loaded with meaning. They go to the heart of a very fundamental disagreement between Christianity and Islam, which, if left unresolved, may substantially undermine the prospects for any real dialogue.[1] It is one thing – and it is a very big thing – to set aside or overcome historical grudges and ignorance; it is another to ascertain if the profoundly different anthropologies in Christianity and Islam meet in a common notion of a human being who possesses "inalienable rights." In Christian anthropology, humans are created in God's image and called to share God's life. Both of these notions are anathema to Islam, which considers them blasphemous.

God and Reason

The single most famous remarks by Pope Benedict XVI about Islam were in the *Regensburg Lecture*. Explaining its most controversial part and the quotation of Emperor Manuel II Paleologus, Benedict said that the section on Islam was part of an overall examination of the "relationship between faith and reason." The emperor had said that spreading faith by the sword is not in accordance with right reason, and that "not acting reasonably is contrary to God's nature." Benedict XVI pointed to this as "the decisive statement in this argument against violent conversion." It is decisive because it presumes that God *is* reason. If He is reason, then it is immoral to employ force against conscience.

It is standard Muslim rhetoric to refer to Judaism and Christianity as Abrahamic faiths. However, the real question is not whether Christianity and Islam share a common origin in Abraham, whom Islam claims as a Muslim, but

---

[1] An illustrative moment of mutual incomprehension came in early 2011, when Benedict XVI protested against the violence and discrimination against Coptic Christians in Egypt after a church bombing left 23 people dead. In response, the president of Al-Azhar University in Cairo, Sheik Ahmad el-Tayeb, and members of the Islamic Research Academy unanimously suspended dialogue with the Vatican, which had been taking place annually since 2000 in the form of meetings of the Joint Committee for Dialogue. Benedict's remarks, according to Sheik el-Tayeb, constituted an "unacceptable interference in Egypt's affairs."

whether or not they share a God who is *Logos* – the Greek word for word or reason. The answer to this question, raised so powerfully by the *Regensburg Lecture*, is really what will determine the possibility and nature of any Catholic-Muslim dialogue. This explains Benedict XVI's preoccupation with freedom of conscience and freedom of religion, and why he was always sure to mention them in any discussion of dialogue with Islam.

Of course, the violent Muslim reactions to Benedict XVI's statements in the *Regensburg Lecture* illustrated the very point he was making, which was that a conception of God without reason, or above reason, leads to that very violence. Is this God without reason Allah? Benedict's allusion to the teachings of 11th century Islamic philosopher Ibn Hazm – "God is not bound even by his own word" – suggests that possibility. However, Benedict was also addressing the attempts in the history of the Catholic Church to strip God of reason. In either case, the interesting term Benedict used to describe this denigration of reason is *dehellenization* – extirpating the gift of Greek philosophy from Christianity or Islam.

As Benedict XVI pointed out, there were strong tendencies within the Church to move in this direction in the teachings of 13th-century theologian Duns Scotus and others. The anti-rational view was violently manifested in the millenarian movements of the Middle Ages, and more peaceably within the movement that was known as fideism – faith alone, based on *sola scriptura*, which became a tenet of Protestantism. In its most radical form, this school held that faith is enough. Forget reason, Greek philosophy, and Thomas Aquinas. However, the anti-rationalist view in its more extreme forms has never predominated in Catholicism, because it was protected by its understanding of the magisterial pronouncement in the Gospel of John that Christ is *Logos*. If Christ is *Logos*, if God introduces himself as *ratio*, then God is not only all-powerful; He is also reason. On the basis of this revelation and Greek philosophy, particularly that of Aristotle, Thomas Aquinas achieved the defining synthesis of reason and revelation in Christianity.

That makes it all the more ironic that an irate Pakistani political leader chose to denounce Benedict XVI in these terms: "He has a dark mentality that comes from the darkness of the Middle Ages." It is curious that the Pakistani should have described this period as one of "darkness," for it was during this era that Islam, not Christianity, took a decisive step away from rationality and chose to dehellenize itself.

The Historical Background of Islamic Theology

This regression began over an argument, already begun in the 8th century, about the status of reason in relationship to God's revelation and omnipotence. The outcome of this struggle in the late 9th century decisively affected the character of the Islamic world. This struggle had its roots in a profound disagreement over who God is. There was a side in this debate that would seem very familiar to Westerners, because it was as deeply influenced by Greek philosophy as was Christianity. In fact, Greek influences reached Islam through its contact with Christianity in the large parts of the Byzantine Empire that it had conquered.

The Mu'tazilite school, composed of the Muslim rationalist theologians, fought for the primacy of reason in Islam. The Mu'tazilites were supported by Caliph al-Ma'mun (786-833), the greatest advocate of Greek thought in Islamic history. It was he, in the famous House of Wisdom (*Bait al Hikma*), who sponsored the translation of the Greek philosophical texts into Arabic. It was said that Aristotle came to him in a dream. In the dream, Al-Ma'mun asked Aristotle, "What is the good?" Aristotle answered, "It is what is rationally good." Al-Ma'mun embraced this answer, and sponsored the first Arab philosopher. This was the period of Islam's hellenization.

The Mu'tazilites held that God is not only power; He is also reason. They emphasized most particularly God's rationality and justice. Human reason is a gift from God, who expects humans to use it to come to know Him. The Mu'tazilites would say: the order in creation, with laws that operate according to the nature of things – "nature" is what makes them what they are – is a manifestation of God's rationality. It is not a constraint upon who He is or what He can do; it is a reflection of who He is. Through reason, humans are able to understand God as manifested in his creation and to apprehend the moral law, which it is incumbent upon them to follow with the gift of their free will. This is true of all people, not just of Muslims. Therefore, as leading Mu'tazilite thinker Abd-al Jabbar said, "It is obligatory for you to carry out what accords with reason." God's justice is intimately related to his rationality, in fact, inseparable from it. He will not require of humans things beyond their powers, and then punish them for not doing them. He will not punish someone for another person's deeds. He will, in fact, reward the obedient and punish the disobedient. God, being reason, would not expect humans to accept anything contrary to it. To do otherwise would be unreasonable and, therefore, unworthy of Him.

There took place a very interesting encounter between two of al-Ma'mun's courtiers, one a Muslim cousin of the caliph, and the other a learned Christian named al-Kindi (not to be confused with the Arab philosopher of that name), that dramatically illustrates the hellenization of Islam. This debate, conducted in letters, is still available in a book, *The Apology of Al Kindi*, or "The Epistle of Abdallah ibn Ismaîl the Hâshimite to Abd al Masîh ibn Ishâc al Kindy, inviting him to embrace Islam; and the reply of Abd al Masîh, refuting the same, and inviting the Hâshimite to embrace the Christian Faith." Al-Ma'mun was said to have been so interested in this exchange that he had the letters read to him without stopping.

Addressed to his Christian adversary, ibn Ismaîl's preamble to the debate is worth quoting at length for what it reveals about the spirit of free inquiry at al-Ma'mun's court and the esteem in which reason was held at the time. Here are the grounds of dialogue set out by the Muslim. The preamble also contains clear references to Mu'tazilite teachings on free will and responsibility.

> Therefore bring forward all the arguments you wish and say what-ever you please and speak your mind freely. Now that you are safe and free to say whatever you please, appoint some arbitrator who will im-partially judge between us and lean only towards the truth and be free from the empery of passion: and that arbitrator shall be reason, whereby God makes us responsible for our own rewards and punishments. Hereby I have dealt justly with you and have given you full security and am ready to accept whatever decision reason may give for me or against me.

The primacy of reason here is explicit. It is interesting to note how closely these remarks accord to the very things for which Benedict XVI was calling in the *Regensburg Lecture*, when he quoted the Byzantine emperor as saying, "Whoever would lead someone to faith needs the ability to speak well and to reason properly, without violence and threats..." Reason, not force, is the arbi-trator, on the grounds of Greek philosophy.

Unfortunately, three caliphs later, the Mu'tazilites were suppressed during the reign of Caliph Ja'afar al-Mutawakkil (847-861), who made holding the Mu'tazilite doctrines a crime punishable by death. The long process of dehell-enization and its resulting ossification began.

The opponents of Mu'tazilites were called the Ash'arites, after al-Ash'ari, who denied all the principal Mu'tazilite tenets. His teachings require detailed attention, because they came to form the general Muslim Arab culture in such a decisive way that, without knowledge of them, much of what is taking place today would be incomprehensible. The prevalence of these teachings affects, as well, the prospects for Catholic-Muslim dialogue.

Al-Ash'ari denied the Mu'tazilite teaching that, through unaided reason, humans can come to know good and evil. He saw two reasons for this. One is that human reason is corrupted by self-interest, and is incapable of knowing anything beyond it. The far more profound reason comes from Ash'arite metaphysics. Al-Ash'ari claimed that there is nothing to be known in terms of moral philosophy, because things are neither good nor bad in themselves. They have no nature, so there is nothing in them that could lead one to discern that this is good, or that is bad.

This idea that things are neither good nor bad in themselves answered for the Ash'arites the famous question that Socrates asked in the *Euthyphro*: do the gods love piety because it is good, or is it good because the gods love it? The Mu'tazilites answered with the former; the Ash'arites answered with the latter. In other words, the Ash'arites would say: God does not forbid murder because it is bad; it is bad because He forbids it. Telling lies is not evil in itself. It is only evil because God says not to lie. However, He could change his mind tomorrow and make lying obligatory. Ibn Hazm, the theologian from Spain, quoted by Benedict XVI, said that God is not bound even by His own word. He also said that God may require acts of idolatry, which would be repugnant to a Muslim, and, if He does, then we must do them without question. God may also choose to reward those who disobey him and punish those who obey him, and there could be no gainsaying Him for doing so. God does what He wills. And whatever He wills is just, because right is the rule of the stronger.

The Ash'arites said that God is absolute power and pure will. God is not bound by anything; God can do anything. He is unaccountable. God is above or without reason; therefore, you cannot use reason to constrain what God may do by some idea of what is just. You cannot say that there is anything unreasonable in what He might do, such as oblige you to engage in ritual murder. His will is what is just by definition, no matter what He wills. Therefore, unlike the Mu'tazilites, the Ash'arites said that revelation in the Qur'an does not reveal what is good and evil; it *constitutes* what is good and evil. Furthermore, it is the sole source of this knowledge.

God is omnipotent to the extent that no other thing is so much as potent. This extends to the denial of secondary causality. For the Ash'arites, there are no secondary causes in creation, no cause and effect in the natural world. There is solely the first and only cause, the prime cause: Allah, who does everything directly. Fire does not burn cotton; God does. Gravity does not make the rock fall; God does. To suggest otherwise would mean that God is not omnipotent, because the secondary causes would exist somehow semi-autonomously, apart from Him.

Therefore, there are no laws of nature that inhere in things themselves and make them what they are. Things have nothing within themselves; they have no nature. They are only momentary juxtapositions of time-space atoms that God has agglomerated in a certain way for the instant, and there is no telling what they may become in the next instant.

Ash'arite metaphysics robs reality of its integrity. It has no standing of its own on which one can rely. One instantaneous expression of God's will is replaced by the next instantaneous expression, with nothing connecting them other than God's determination. Everything is miraculous. As a result, things become incomprehensible. Reason loses its purchase on reality.

God, in turn, becomes a legal positivist. In Aristotelian terms, justice is giving to things what is due them according to what they are. In other words, in order to act justly, one must first know what things are. It is exactly this knowledge that the Ash'arites said is unavailable to humans. You cannot know what things are in themselves, because there is no "in themselves." Because of this, a work such as Aristotle's *The Ethics*, the essential work of moral philosophy, would be impossible. Reality is unknowable, and there is nothing to be known. The primacy of reason is replaced by the primacy of will and force.

It was in the "darkness" of the Middle Ages, to which Benedict's Pakistani critic alluded, that the *coup de grace* to philosophy was delivered by Abu Hamid al-Ghazali (1058-1111), perhaps the single most influential Muslim thinker after Muhammad. As a good Ash'arite, al-Ghazali vehemently rejected Greek thought: "The source of their [the Mu'tazilites' and Muslim philosophers'] infidelity was their hearing terrible names such as Socrates and Hippocrates, Plato and Aristotle." With his work on *The Incoherence of the Philosophers*, the extirpation of philosophy from the Muslim world was practically complete. Al-Ghazali spoke of "the mind which, once it testifies to the truthfulness of the Prophet, must cease to act." Over the following centuries, as a consequence of these teachings, it gradually ceased to act, and Muslim culture grew increasingly dysfunctional as a result.

To give an indication of how prevalent Ash'arite thinking became, here is a quote from a 15th-century thinker, Mohammed Yusuf as-Sanusi. He is simply repeating the doctrines that developed in the 9th century: "It is impossible for the Most High to determine an act as obligatory or forbidden for the sake of any objective, since all acts are equal in that they are his creation and production. Therefore, the specification of certain acts as obligatory and others as forbidden or with any other determination takes place by his pure choice, which has no cause. Intelligibility has no place at all in it; rather it can be known only by revealed law (shari'a)."

"Intelligibility has no place in it." God does not act for reasons. God is not ordered teleologically; He can do anything. Since God acts for no reasons, what he does is not intelligible and cannot be understood. You cannot come to know God, all you come to know is his revelation, which is why al-Ghazali's teacher, al-Juwayni, taught that "there is nothing obligatory by reason." And al-Ghazali repeated that "no obligations flow from reason, but from the Shari'a." This, of course, is the antithesis of al-Jabbar's statement that "it is obligatory for you to carry out what accords with reason." The difference in the status of reason could not be starker or of greater consequence.

The Ash'arite strain of thinking can be traced through the centuries to the present day. The triumph of the Ash'arite school over the Mu'tazilite so influenced the Muslim world, particularly in the Middle East, that the development of science was stillborn, the translation efforts were curtailed, philosophy was banned, and theology degenerated into the enumeration of divine shari'a rules for everything. The principle of Islamic jurisprudence became "reason is not a legislator." Education devolved into *taqlid*: imitation and memorization. Some Sunni Muslims explicitly acknowledge this loss. For instance, in one of his last interviews, King Hussein of Jordon was asked by journalist Milton Viorst, "Would you agree that the Muslim decline can be dated from the 9th century when Islam missed the chance to become the religion of reason and moderation by crushing the Mu'tazilite movement?" King Hussein answered, "That is essentially correct, and we must do what we can to change that now." In any case, the Muslim mind closed in a profound way. The effects of this closure pervade the Muslim world to this day, and present enormous obstacles to Catholic-Muslim dialogue.

How do we think about the common good and justice with the mental horizon so circumscribed? If the common good and justice are solely defined by revelation, and the revelations differ, how can mutual ground be found? If nothing is obligatory by reason, what will act as an arbitrator in the dialogue? How, with the loss of philosophy, epistemology and ethics, can we reason together? Without these disciplines, it is hard to envisage upon what basis meaningful interfaith dialogue with Islam could take place. It is precisely because of these deeply embedded problems that Benedict XVI called for a re-hellenization of Islam (and the West), so that both recognize reason as capable of apprehending reality. Is a re-hellenization of Islam possible, with Allah as *Logos*? The violent reaction to Pope Benedict's Regensburg speech was not a hopeful harbinger.

Contemporary Muslim Responses

However, there were other, more thoughtful reactions, which came from a broad range of Muslim thinkers. On October 12, 2006, 38 Muslim scholars and clerics published an *Open Letter to the Pope* criticizing his stance on Islam, with alleged corrections to some of his supposed misstatements in the *Regensburg Lecture*. More significantly, in October, 2007, 138 Islamic leaders, clerics and intellectuals, organized by the Royal Aal al-Bayt Institute for Islamic Thought,[2] Amman, Jordan, addressed a lengthy letter to Benedict XVI and other Christian leaders, titled "A Common Word between Us and You." While the first letter was a critique, the second was a proposal.

Since there is no body or institution representing all Muslims, or even all Sunni Muslims, partners in dialogue are often government-appointed scholars, leaders of specific spiritual groups, or individual academics with no particular following in the Islamic world. It is, therefore, particularly notable that the signatories to this letter were so broadly representative of Islam in general, and included both Sunni and Shi'a clerics and scholars from 40 countries. It is a remarkable assemblage. This, then, is a very important document – indeed, there has not been anything like it before – as it seems to be considered from the Muslim side the foundation stone for dialogue with Christians. It is therefore necessary to pay close attention to what it says.

The inspiration for the title of the letter comes from the following passage in the Qur'an, which is quoted in the opening portion of the letter: "Say: O People of the Scripture! Come to a common word between us and you: that we shall worship none but God, and that we shall ascribe no partner unto Him, and that none of us shall take others for lords beside God. And if they turn away, then say: Bear witness that we are they who have surrendered (unto Him)" (Aal 'Imran 3:64).

The Qur'anic phrase in its title, *kalima-tun sawa* ("a common word"), has been interpreted by Muslims in a number of ways. Muhammad's proselytizing challenge to the Christians of Najran provides the general context for its use. One of the main interpretations emphasizes the need for conversion to Islam. Zeki Saritoprak, who holds the B. S. Nursi Chair in Islamic Studies at John Carroll University, points out that "an initiative which chooses this phrase as its title, therefore, should be conscious of this context. Some contemporary Muslim

---

2 According to Dr. Patrick Sookhdeo of Barnabas Fund, "This organisation seeks to solidify an international, interdenominational body of Muslim religious scholars to represent the interests of Islam to governments, other religions and international bodies."

writers insist that those who interpret *kalima-tun sawa* without this emphasis on conversion are, in fact, distorting and corrupting the meaning of the text." This is not the only interpretation, but the point is that the Christian reader should be aware that things are not always what they first seem on the surface. A Muslim can see the same word and understand it differently.

The letter is extremely interesting in that, unlike the preamble to al-Kindi, it does not address the status of reason at all. In fact, the word "reason" does not appear, except in the participle "reasoning," which is taken from a quote from the Gospel of Mark. There is nothing in the letter that approximates ibn Ismaîl's suggestion of reason as the arbitrator of the dialogue. Rather, the letter presents itself as an exegesis of Qur'anic and Christian scriptures, an endeavor that comports with the Islamic perspective of *sola scriptura*. While it is not unusual for Muslims to explicate their own Scripture, an interpretive task or commentary called *tafsir*, it is somewhat unusual for them to present themselves as exegetes of the Old and New Testaments, both of which the Qur'an claims were corrupted or falsified. It is on the basis of their scriptural readings that the authors of the letter conclude that Muslims and Christians can construct a future based upon "peace and justice between the two religious communities." This would seem to be a hopeful sign.

According to the letter, this can be achieved because "the very foundational principles of both faiths [are] love of the One God, and love of the neighbor." This sounds very appealing. The rest of the letter attempts to demonstrate that these virtues are similarly understood in both forms of scripture. It is particularly interesting to note that the efforts to find "a Common Word" are exclusively based upon revelation, which, as mentioned earlier, mirrors the majority conception within Islam that only revelation provides certain knowledge or has authenticity. It is important, then, to know the Muslim understanding of revelation. In Islam, the Qur'an was directly dictated by God, word for word in Arabic, through the Angel Gabriel to Muhammad. It is God's literal, uncreated word, without any influence on it from Muhammad as its transmitter. The Qur'an has existed coeternally with Allah in heaven exactly as it exists today. It is not historically, culturally, or linguistically contingent on the circumstances of its revelation.

In an interview in 2003, Fr. Maurice Borrmans, a Vatican pioneer in interreligious dialogue with Muslims and, at that time, a professor at the Pontifical Institute of Arabic Studies, pointed to the profound ramifications of this understanding of revelation: "On the Muslim side, however, it is maintained that the Koran is a book entirely dictated and revealed by Allah through Mohammed and, therefore, it is not possible to exercise a scientific-critical approach... This is the origin of the misunderstanding between the different points of view. The transcendence that is God's has been attributed to the Koran, and then to the society and to the Shariah [Islamic law]. While such characteristics persist, the dialogue will be difficult..."[3]

Therefore, because of the unique authority of Islamic Scripture, everything relies on the accuracy of its interpretation. In respect to the love of God and the love of the neighbor, the first two sections of the letter first present what the Qur'an or the *hadith* (the accounts of what Muhammad said or did) say, and then what the Bible professes.

In order to understand the references to Allah in the letter, one must first know the main Islamic teachings regarding Him, which emphasize above all monotheism: that He is one. The unity of God, *tawhid*, is the principal doctrine of Islam. Muslims, therefore, deplore the notion of the Trinity and the Incarnation. The Trinity is never mentioned in the letter. Yet almost every citation in the letter from the Qur'an regarding the unity of Allah includes the repeated assertions that "He hath no associate" or that "He hath no partner." The letter offers the anodyne interpretation that this means Muslims "must love God uniquely." This is certainly so, but these are all obvious and standard references to Islam's emphatic denial of the Trinity and the Incarnation.

The inscriptions on the Dome of the Rock, the oldest historical record of Muslim doctrine (AD 691), repeatedly make clear that God has no son, meaning no "associate" or "partner." It is certainly polite for the authors of the letter not to have mentioned the main meaning of these phrases, but it is also close to astonishing, if not audacious, to find their frequent repetition. The word "associate" appears eight times in the main text, and six times in the notes; the word "partner" appears seven times in the main text. In a letter, the purported purpose of which is not to point out the essential differences between Islam and Christianity, but their similarities, this is conspicuous. For anyone familiar with Islam, there are 15 reminders in the main text – one might even say admonishments – that the Trinity is false and that Christ is not the son of God.[4]

Who, then, is the One God whom Christians are invited to acknowledge in a shared monotheism with Islam? The principal Muslim doctrine concerning

---

[3] http://www.zenit.org/article-6874?l=english

[4] Revulsion at the idea of the Incarnation is expressed many times in the Qur'an. Here is one example in Surah 19:88–91: "And they say, 'The Most Merciful has taken [for Himself] a son.' You have done an atrocious thing. The heavens almost rupture therefrom and the Earth splits open and the mountains collapse in devastation that they attribute to the Most Merciful a son." See also Surah 112. In Sahih Muslim (156), "When asked, 'Which sin is the gravest in the eyes of Allah?" he [Muhammad] replies: 'That you associate a partner with Allah.'"

God beside *tawhid* is called *tanzih*, meaning God's infinite transcendence to humans and his utter inaccessibility. There is a famous, emblematic saying in Arabic: *bila kayfa wala tashbih* (without asking how and without comparing). Never compare anything to Allah; do not compare humans to Him; do not compare Him to anything in creation, because He is incomparable. As German Muslim Murad Wilfried Hofmann states, "He remains unfathomable, unimaginable, unseizable, incomprehensible, indescribable." For humans, there can be no familial relationship to God. It would be considered blasphemous to address Him as Father or to refer to oneself as a child of God. The name that signifies the ideal relationship between God and humans is Abdullah, which joins *'abd* (slave) with Allah (God), meaning "slave of God."

In Genesis, humans are made in the image and likeness of God. In the Qur'an, they are not made in God's image or likeness. This has enormous ramifications. "Progress," President Barack Obama said in his June, 2009 speech at Al-Azhar theological university in Cairo, "does not come when we demonize enemies... It comes when we look into the eyes of the other and see the face of God." This is a particularly Christian reflection, which no orthodox Sunni Muslim in his audience could have accepted at the theological level,[5] but it is not an exclusively religious one. Archbishop Celestino Migliore, Apostolic Nuncio and Permanent Observer of the Holy See to the United Nations, wrote in 2007 that "the dialogue we have to establish with the Islamic community is not a matter of reconciling our theological tenets. Rather, it is a matter of agreeing upon the human dignity of every person, created in the image and likeness of God, which greatly precedes one's religious affiliation. From that point on, we can talk to each other and cooperate for the common good." In other words, Archbishop Migliore suggests that knowledge of the divine image in humanity is not exclusive to religion, but actually "precedes" it. The only way in which it could precede it would be through philosophical reflection, as in the Greek discovery of *logos*. The problem here is a double one. Not only is the idea of "the image of God" in humanity a blasphemous one in Islamic revelation, as already mentioned, but mainstream Sunni Islam does not acknowledge or allow a philosophical precedent to itself that would provide for the independent recog-

---

[5] At an inter-faith Iftar dinner during Ramadan (2011), a rabbi and an evangelical preacher both spoke movingly of everyone being made in the image of God. The Sunni imam also spoke movingly, but not in these words. I asked him afterwards and in private if he, too, as a Muslim could proclaim that humans were made in the image and likeness of God. He blanched, but recovered by simply saying that we were all equally made by God. Yes, but that is not the same thing.

nition of "the human dignity of every human being, independent from his or her religious affiliation" for which the archbishop calls. This makes the establishment of the "common good" at this level extremely difficult.

The "Common Word" letter emphasizes two particular things about the one God that will not surprise a student of Ash'arite theology: His power and His sovereignty. In relationship to God, the word "power" appears 11 times in the main text and seven times in the notes. The word "sovereignty" is used 12 times in the main text and six times in the notes. God's power and sovereignty are absolute. He is omnipotent, so much so that "ye cannot harm Him at all." Allah is impervious to humans (Q 9:39). "He is able to do all things" (Q 67:1). "He hath power over all things" (Q 64:1), What is more, though this is left unsaid in the letter, God's sovereignty in Islam is exclusive. Humans are not sovereign; nor do they share in God's sovereignty. This theology has obvious implications for political order.

This omnipotent God is not love, nor does the letter suggest that He is, though God may bestow love, or more appropriately, His favor or affection, upon "those who believe and do good works" (Q 19:96). Certainly, God does not "love" as a matter of necessity. He may bestow his favor as He wills. There is good reason, as was later developed in Muslim theology, for this omission of God as love. Al-Ghazali, for instance, speaks only of humans' love for God (which is in itself a problem since God is unknown; if you cannot know God, how can you love him?), not of God's love for humans. Love is a particularly problematic attribute for Allah to possess because it places Him in relation to a contingent being. How can a totally transcendent Being love a creature infinitely below Him? How can God desire?

"When there is love," said al-Ghazali, "there must be in the lover a sense of incompleteness; a recognition that the beloved is needed for complete realization of the self." For God this is impossible, as He is complete in Himself. "The love of God means that he removes the veil from the heart of man; that God wills and has willed, from all eternity, that man should know Him, and that God causes man to know Him. There is no reaching out on the part of God. He only affects man so that man turns and goes out to Him; there can be no change in God; no development in Him; no supplying of a lack in Himself. He only affects man so that man comes to God." Despite the many citations in the Qur'an about God's love for his obedient servants, this must be understood as God's predilection, an expression of his will. He may *favor* humans when we obey Him, but He does not love us in the Christian sense of *agape*, an overflowing, unconditional divine love. This is completely foreign to mainstream Islam, if not to Sufism.

A contemporary expression of this doctrine is found in a paper by the German convert to Islam, Dr. Murad Wilfried Hofmann, written in 2007 for the Royal Aal al-Bayt Institute for Islamic Thought, in preparation for the composition of the "Common Word" letter. Hofmann states that "love establishes a longing and dependency between the lover and the loved one that is irreconcilable with God." Loving his creation is "incompatible with the very nature of God as sublime and totally self-sufficient." Hofmann concludes that "it is safer and more accurate not to speak of 'love' when addressing His clemency, compassion, benevolence, goodness, or mercy."

Therefore, the intimation of "A Common Word" that Muslims and Christians worship and love the same God is highly problematic. It is important to note that *Nostra Aetate,* in affirming that "They [the Muslims] adore the one God," does not suggest that it is the *same* God. A God forever alone in his absolute power is not identical to a God of love who is in eternal relationship with Himself in the Trinity of three Persons. The favor of an inscrutable God is different from the love of a God who makes Himself known. As Benedict XVI said, "God is not solitude, but perfect communion. For this reason the human person, the image of God, realizes himself or herself in love, which is a sincere gift of self" (Angelus, Solemnity of the Most Holy Trinity, Sunday, May 22, 2005). Unfortunately, because of these profound theological differences, this statement is not, and cannot be, "a common word" with Islam.

If the love of God is different in the two faiths, what about the "love of the neighbor" that the letter asserts is a foundational principle of both? Here, again, the authors provide texts to illustrate the necessity and paramount importance of love of neighbor. However, there are *no* Qur'anic citations confirming this injunction, though there are many admonitions in the Qur'an regarding charity. The confirmatory quotations in the letter come only from the *hadith*, one of which quotes Muhammad as saying, "None of you has faith until you love for your neighbor what you love for your self" (Sahih Muslim, Kitab al-Iman, 67-1, *hadith* no. 45). The letter then provides citations from Matthew and Mark that "you shall love your neighbor as yourself."

However, the letter nowhere addresses the definition of who one's neighbor is. In Christianity, the parable of the Good Samaritan makes the answer clear. The human family is universal; our relationship as brothers and sisters is based on the image of God in every person. There is no equivalent to this in the Qur'an, which states, "believers are naught else than brothers," but *only* believers are brothers (49:10). In fact, within Islam, one's neighbor is invariably understood to be a fellow Muslim. Fr. Samir Khalil Samir, the Egyptian Jesuit scholar of Islam, has pointed out that the Arabic text of the letter uses the word *jar* for neighbor, which means someone in geographic proximity, rather than the Christian Arabic word, *qarib*, which means a broader family relationship not based on geography. While the requirements of charitable giving, of the care for orphans and widows, and of the needy, is an impressive part of the Muslim faith, these obligations apply only to other Muslims and, in Islamic jurisprudence, the utilization of *Zakat* (charitable funds) for non-Muslims is not permitted.

In other words, strictly speaking, there is no such thing as a non-Muslim neighbor in Islam: certainly not *Mushrikun*, or polytheists, Jews, Christians, pagans and all other non-Muslims. The Islamic principle is *al-Walaa' wa'l-Baraa'* (loyalty and friendship towards Muslims, disavowal and enmity towards *kuffar*, the unbelievers). The letter mentions none of this, leaving open the impression that the word "neighbor" means the same thing in both faiths.

Recently, Saudi Shaykh al-'Ulwan expressed this attitude in *Al-Tibyan – Sharh Nawaqid al-Islam*, which states that "The aiding and supporting of polytheists is a great perturbing sedition that has now become widespread... it has reached out and captured hearts, all of them beguiled by the polytheists, especially in our time... In my view this is due to a general failure to study the Islamic legal sciences, and to the readiness to study Greek science and philosophy – God preserve us! – whereby things that are permitted have become prohibited, and things prohibited permitted."

Unfortunately, the absence of the "image of God" in humanity removes the concept of a universal human family from Islam. As Surah 5:51 states: "O you who believe! Take not the Jews and the Christians as Auliya' (allies), they are but Auliya' to one another. And if any amongst you takes them as Auliya', then surely he is one of them. Verily, Allah guides not those people who are the Zalimun (polytheists and wrong-doers and unjust)." Indeed, according to the Qur'an, the basis of relations between the believers and the unbelievers is to be one of lasting enmity: Surah 60:4: "Indeed there has been an excellent example for you in Ibrahim (Abraham) and those with him, when they said to their people: 'Verily, we are free from you and whatever you worship besides Allah, we have rejected you, and there has started between us and you, hostility and hatred for ever, until you believe in Allah alone.'" The Christian notion of loving one's enemies is completely foreign to Islam.

What is the "peace and justice between the two religious communities" of which "A Common Word" speaks? As we have seen, there is no common conception of "justice" since the term is reduced in Islam to the jurisprudential stipulations of shari'a. It is intriguing to note the exact similarities between the "Common Word" and the letter Muhammad supposedly sent to Emperor Heraclius (its authenticity is disputed): "Say (O Muhammad): 'O people of the scripture! Come to a word common to you and us that we worship none but Allah and that we associate nothing in worship with Him, and that none of us shall take others as Lords beside Allah.' Then, if they turn away, say: 'Bear witness that we are Muslims' (those who have surrendered to Allah)" (3:64). The full text of the letter gives the context for this same Qur'anic citation; it is a call for submission to Islam.

The point here is not to suspect the good will of the Muslim interlocutors, but to give some idea of the mental universe from which they are speaking so that their vocabulary can be properly understood or, at least, not misunderstood. Therefore, one must see from their perspective exactly how broad or narrow the concept of the neighbor is. One thing that it does not entail is the notion of human equality that undergirds the Western notion of democracy and inalienable human rights.

In *The Crisis of Islamic Civilization*, Ali Allawi, a distinguished former minister of both finance and defense in the new Iraq, writes that, "The entire edifice of individual rights derived from the natural state of the individual or through a secular ethical or political theory is alien to the structure of Islamic reasoning." The end result, as Allawi says, is that the question of human rights does not even arise within the Muslim mind.

Nothing makes clearer how un-Islamic the notion of equality is than *The Cairo Declaration on Human Rights in Islam,* signed by 45 foreign ministers of the Organization of the Islamic Conference on August 5, 1990. The Cairo Declaration was issued as an appendix to the *UN Universal Declaration of Human Rights* to make explicit Muslim differences with the UN Declaration, which espouses universal, equal rights. The last two articles in the Cairo Declaration state that "All rights and freedoms stipulated in this Declaration are subject to the Islamic *Shari'a*," (Article 24) and that "The Islamic *Shari'a* is the only source of reference for the explanation or clarification [of] any of the articles of this Declaration" (Article 25). Elsewhere it declares that "no one in principle has the right to suspend ... or violate or ignore its [Islam's] commandments, in as much as they are binding divine commandments, which are contained in the Revealed Books of God and were sent through the last of His Prophets... Every person is individually responsible – and the Ummah collectively responsible – for their safeguard."

Under the dispensation of shari'a, what does respect for human rights look like? In June, 2000, the then grand sheikh of Al-Azhar, the highest jurisprudential authority of the Sunni world, the late Mohammed Sayed Tantawi, offered Saudi Arabia as the model. He said, "Saudi Arabia leads the world in the protection of human rights because it protects them according to the *shari'a* of

God... Everyone knows that Saudi Arabia is the leading country for the application of human rights in Islam in a just and objective fashion, with no aggression and no prejudice." This is a stunning statement, because as Dr. Muhammad al-Houni, a Libyan intellectual living in Italy, said, "Islamic law was not familiar with equality or civil rights, because it was a product of its times." How then is shari'a the protector?

Shari'a does not contain the concept of citizenship, for which there was no word in Arabic. Shari'a codifies the inequality between Muslims and non-Muslims, and between men and women. In its terms, these inequalities appear to be unbridgeable. This is evident from the rigid discrimination against non-Muslims in Saudi Arabia, a shari'a state, to say nothing of the state of subjection in which women are kept. Islam is considered the *din al-fitra*, the religion that is "natural" to humans. It was Adam's religion and would be everyone's religion were they not converted as children to apostasy in their upbringing by Christians, Jews, Hindus, or others. Therefore, restoring everyone to Islam is the only means to true "equality." Benedict XVI clearly understood this problematic aspect of Islam, which is why he insisted upon *universal* human rights as the path to equality for non-Muslims.

We can now understand more fully why there is no notion of inalienable human rights in Islam or a notion of freedom of conscience. In Arabic there was, according to the pioneer scholar of Islam, Ignaz Goldziher, no word for "conscience."[6] So if one wonders why there was no freedom of conscience in Islam – in fact, there is no freedom of conscience in Islam today – one simply asks: how can there be freedom of something for which there was not even a word? If there is no word for it, how can it be known? Since reason has been degraded, bereft of the ability to know good and evil, what possible relevance could conscience have? It would not serve any function. This does not mean Islam is without a moral sense. It simply means that this moral sense exclusively comes from revelation, and one's conscience, based upon reason, has no authority whatsoever. That is why the single most important study in Islam is of Islamic jurisprudence, which regulates every single aspect of life. In Islamic jurisprudence, there is a principle that states, "reason is not a legislator." Within the metaphysical and epistemological view of Islam, conscience would be useless. This makes dialogue difficult.

This also helps explain why Benedict XVI was so insistent on mentioning freedom of conscience and religion whenever he met with Muslims or dis-

---

[6] *Damir* does not literally mean "conscience", though it is widely used to mean that today.

cussed dialogue with them. He clearly understood that these are the very things that Islam, as it currently understands itself in the majority expression of the faith, is unable to give. Yet he insisted on this as the necessary ground for dialogue. The essential issue here, as mentioned before, is the status of reason, which is why the latest forum in the official Vatican Catholic-Muslim dialogue was so important. The forum's subject was "Reason, Faith, and Mankind." Can we reason together? Benedict XVI's answer was that this is possible only in so far as we and they are hellenized, which means that both sides recognize reason as capable of apprehending reality.

Is this the case in the current dialogue? In November, 2011, 24 Catholic and 24 Muslim leaders, scholars, and educators met on the east bank of the Jordan River for the second of the two Catholic-Muslim Forums inaugurated by Benedict XVI in 2008 to encourage dialogue. Jordan's King Abdullah saluted the participants: "the forum is the outcome of ongoing initiatives to foster concepts embraced by both Muslims and Christians." There certainly are things in common, principally in morals but, as we have seen, the sources of those morals differ significantly in terms of the authority on which they draw.

On the Muslim side, Ibrahim Kalin, a Turkish philosopher, said, "Islam largely shares this notion of rationality with Judaism and Christianity." According to *The Tablet*, he claimed that "the Qur'an teaches a natural law that would be quite familiar to Thomists. Charges of irrationality persist, he said, because Islam kept a balance of faith and reason while the Enlightenment tipped the focus of Western thought towards reason and science."

Would that this were so; then there could be a very deep dialogue indeed. Unfortunately, Kalin omitted to say that the one Muslim theological school that roughly fits his description, the Mu'tazilites, was irreparably crushed, as mentioned earlier, starting around the year 850 AD. This began the period of de-hellenization to which Pope Benedict referred. Since then, the vast majority of Muslims have rejected the existence of natural law.

Another Muslim scholar present at the November dialogue was Aref Ali Nayed, a Libyan theologian, who played an important role in his country's revolution and who now serves as Tripoli's ambassador in the United Arab Emirates. He is a former Professor at the Pontifical Institute for Arabic and Islamic Studies. In respect to the Arab Spring, he has cautioned that "Such movements must be guided by the light of faith, but reasoned faith that encourages thinking and dialogue." Nayed is a very well-educated, thoughtful man, who was also one of the prime movers behind and one of the signatories of "A Common Word," as well as the chief spokesman on its behalf.

In 2006, he also issued his own very detailed and critical response to Benedict's *Regensburg Lecture*. It is worth paying attention to, because Nayed is not some crude fundamentalist, but a Muslim intellectual of considerable stature. He professes to be "a devout Sunni Muslim theologian of the Ash'arite school." His critique reveals how deeply embedded Ash'arite views are even today and the limits of how far an Ash'arite Muslim can go in dialogue with a Christian. This is important because, despite all the varieties of Islam, Ash'arism remains the majority view. It is therefore necessary to know exactly what these limitations are.

Nayed takes issue with Benedict XVI's statement that "not to act in accordance to reason is contrary to God's nature." He claims that this statement is "very complex" and that it invites a false contrast between a supposedly reasonable Christianity and a supposedly unreasonable Islam. To correct this impression, Nayed comes to the defense of Ibn Hazm, of all people, from whom even the authors of the *Open Letter to the Pope* tried to distance themselves. He says that "Reason as a gift from God can never be above God. That is the whole point of Ibn Hazm; a point that was paraphrased in such a mutilated way by Benedict XVI's learned sources. Ibn Hazm, like the Asha'rite theologians with whom he often contended, did insist upon God's absolute freedom to act. However, Ibn Hazm did recognize, like most other Muslim theologians that God freely chooses, in His compassion towards His creatures, to self-consistently act reasonably so that we can use our reason to align ourselves with His guidance and directive." In this statement, Nayed seems to be avoiding the somewhat obvious obverse of the proposition that, if God freely chooses to act reasonably, He can also choose freely to act unreasonably, which is the whole point of Benedict's objection to this theological view. This is what "absolute freedom to act" *means*, and what it has to mean if reason is not in God's essence.

Nayed goes on to say that "Ibn Hazm, like most other Muslim theologians did hold that God is not externally-bound by anything, including reason. However, at no point does Ibn Hazm claim that God does not *freely* self-commit Himself and honors such commitments... Reason need not be above God, and externally normative to Him. It can be a grace of God that is normative because of God's own free commitment to acting consistently with it."

This statement, again, avoids the implications of what is really being said. There is only one way that reason could be normative, and that is if God is *Logos*. If reason is somehow external to God, whether above or below Him, it cannot be essentially normative. It then simply becomes optional, and acting against it is not necessarily wrong. Also, what Ibn Hazm actually claims is made clear in his *Kitab al-Fisal* (*Detailed Critical Examination*), where he says of God that "He judges as He pleases and whatever He judges is just." Ibn Hazm insists that "whatever" can mean anything: "if God the Exalted had informed us that He would punish us for the acts of others ... or for our own obedience, all that would have been right and just, and we should have been obliged to accept it." This of course is consistent with the Ash'arite view of God as pure will, and completely contrary to the view that He is reason and justice.

Nayed also objects that "Most major Christian theologians, even the reason-loving Aquinas never put reason above God." This is a straw-man argument. The point of Aquinas and Benedict XVI is not that reason is above God, but that God *is* reason by His nature. However, this position disturbs Nayed, because "talk of the 'nature' of God is itself problematic." Why is this so? Though it is left unsaid in his commentary, the reason it is problematic for an Ash'arite is that a God of pure will *cannot* be known. He is epistemologically unavailable. And what He wills can be known only in so far as He chooses to disclose it in revelation. In fact, this is all that Allah reveals – His rules – but not Himself.

Nayed also shows his sympathy with the voluntarists in the history of Catholic theology, like Duns Scotus, whom Benedict criticized in the *Regensburg Lecture*. Nayed states that "Muslim theologians were not alone in caring about the affirmation of God's sovereignty against human pretensions to govern Him with human criteria." This is another revealing statement, as it suggests that human knowledge of God is nothing other than pretension. Of course, humans think with "human criteria." Does that exclude human ability to reason about God? Is there really such a profound fissure between the human mind and God? Is not God the source of intellect in both revelation *and* reason? And is the statement that "God cannot act unjustly because He is by nature just" an attempt "to govern him," or to know Him? It is a peculiarity of this form of Islam that its notion of God's greatness requires the denigration of the human mind.

In *The Consolation of Philosophy*, Boethius, as he was awaiting execution by Emperor Theodoric in the early 6th century, wrote most movingly that "the human soul, in essence, enjoys its highest freedom when it remains in the contemplation of God's mind." This quintessentially Christian reflection assumes that the origin of the human soul is God's mind and that its final end, the good of the mind, must be the truth of God Himself. The difference with Ash'arite Islam is that, within it, one could not contemplate God's mind, but solely His will. This is the defining difference that cuts through the heart of Catholic-Muslim dialogue.

Prospects for Dialogue

What is revealed here and in other Catholic-Muslim dialogues, as mentioned before, is the profound problem of the ontological status of reason. Unless reason is embedded in God's very being, unless He is *Logos,* humans would not be able to apprehend "the laws of Nature and of Nature's God." Such statements would be pure pretension, as would be the assertion that humans have inalienable rights, such as freedom of conscience and religion.

In conversation with a student in Rome, Benedict XVI made a statement that neatly summarizes the core of what is at stake for both Islam and the Catholic Church in any future dialogue. I will omit only one word from it, indicated by empty brackets. He said that "There are only two options. Either one recognizes the priority of reason, of creative Reason that is at the beginning of all things and is the principle of all things – the priority of reason is also the priority of freedom – or one holds the priority of the irrational, inasmuch as everything that functions on our earth and in our lives would be only accidental, marginal, an irrational result – reason would be a product of irrationality. One cannot ultimately 'prove' either project, but the great option of [ ] is the option for rationality and for the priority of reason. This seems to me to be an excellent option, which shows us that behind everything is a great Intelligence to which we can entrust ourselves."

Of course, the missing word in the bracket is "Christianity." The question is whether the word "Islam" could be inserted in its stead and the statement still be read correctly. Does Islam still have the option open for the priority of reason? As we have seen, it most certainly attempted to exercise that option under the Mu'tazilites at a time generally acknowledged as being the apogee of Arab Islamic culture. One could have substituted the word "Islam" at that time, and the statement above would otherwise have stood unaltered as an expression of Mu'tazilite beliefs.

There are Muslim thinkers today who are attempting something similar. There is a new venue in which to see what they have to say: the website Almuslih.org (the reformer). (It is in both Arabic and English.) There, some of the most brilliant minds in the Arab world, such as writer Sayyid al-Qimny, Abd al-Hamid al-Ansari, the former Dean of Islamic Law at Qatar University, and Hassan Mneimneh, director of the Iraq Memory Foundation, and others address the situation today and what must be done to secure a democratic future with human rights. Invariably, they address the problem of the Islamic culture and cult from which it has come.

These reformers included the recently deceased Tunisian philosopher Lafif Lakhdar, one of the brightest lights in the Muslim world, who called for "an acceptance of the division between the domains of faith and politics." He also stated that a reformed Islam "ends the conception of the world divided up into an Abode of Islam destined for expansion and an Abode of War destined for 'Jihad unto the end of time,' as al-Bukhari's *hadith* has it." Lakhdar said forthrightly, "our faith today constitutes a part of the problem, and it is incumbent upon us to reform it, in the school of religious rationalism, so that we turn it into a part of the solution."

An article titled *Freedom and the Progress of Civilization*, by Mohammed al-Sanduk, avers that the greatest scientific and cultural achievements of the Arab Muslim world occurred during, and because of, the ascendancy of the rational theologians, the Mu'tazilites, whose thinking "laid emphasis on the freedom of choice and on the responsibilities that accompany this." Likewise, its decline resulted because of their suppression.

Hasan Hanafi, chairman of the philosophy department at Cairo University, writes that "no real change can take place if there is not a change in the mindset first." This is the reason, he says, that prior efforts at reform have failed, because they "started with social, political and economic structures rather than with inherited intellectual substructures, which remained unchanged even as liberal, western enlightenment-derived structure was superimposed over them." This has not worked because "the imported freedom therefore perches on an infrastructure of inherited fatalism, while the imported Rights of Man sit atop a substructure of the inherited Rights of God, in the same way that the imported sciences are superimposed over an infrastructural legacy of miracles." As this brilliantly insightful sentence implies, the real problem is theological, and it is at this level that reform must take place and real dialogue be held.

It is with these Muslims and those like them that there should be intense dialogue, and it is their influence we should hope to spread by insisting, as did Benedict XVI, on the priority of reason. As for the others, the Muslim fideists for whom scripture alone is legitimate knowledge, how much can be gained from such encounters is hard to say. It is very clear that their Allah of pure will and power is not the God of love and *Logos*. But the extremely astute Fr. Samir Khalil Samir has said, "Dialogue is better than indifference and reciprocal silence." As long as the conversations are kept respectful and honest, even the defining differences can illuminate the landscape.

Dialogue in the U.S.

With this background in mind, we can now examine how Catholic-Muslim dialogue has been conducted in the United States and to what effect. In a paper on interreligious dialogue, Cardinal Jean-Louis Tauran asked: what is dialogue? He answered, "it is the search for an inter-understanding between two individuals with a view to a common interpretation of their agreement or disagreement. It implies a common language, honesty in the presentation of one's position, and the desire to do one's utmost to understand the other's point of view." This is a modest but essential precondition. It seems to be generally shared by some of the American Muslim interlocutors in dialogue. For instance, Muzammil Siddiqi, the co-chairman of the West Coast Dialogue of Catholics and Muslims, said at a meeting in 2001 that "in dialogue, one must speak the truth, be sincere and assume that the other person is also sincere and telling the truth... We may differ on the issues of faith and practices, but we should never misrepresent each other's faith. We should not be involved in distorting the teachings of other faiths and defaming other people."

Both sides agree that there should be no misrepresentations of the other faith. One would assume that this means no misrepresentations of one's own faith, as well. So let us accept this as a standard and measure what is said against it, keeping in mind the vital importance of a common language, meaning words that signify the same things to both sides in the dialogue. As we have already seen from the text of "A Common Word," what might be taken for intentional misrepresentation is often due to the substantially different meaning of words in the context of different cultures. Christian ignorance of the Islamic context can lead to serious misunderstanding of what Muslims are actually saying. Dr. John Borelli, who was the associate director of the Secretariat for Ecumenical and Interreligious Affairs at the United States Conference of Catholic Bishops (USCCB) for 16 years, sagely advised that "There is a need for each side to comprehend as much as possible and understand correctly the beliefs of the other side in their own terms." As one might imagine, this can take a lifetime of learning to do correctly.

The USCCB has been the principal sponsor of Catholic-Muslim dialogue. Each of its three regional bishops' conferences, the Mid-Atlantic, the Midwest, and the West Coast, has undertaken annual dialogues beginning, respectively, in 1998, 1996, and 2000. As one might imagine from so many exchanges, there is some variety in the subject matter, if not in the personnel actually conducting the dialogue. Sometimes, a single topic which requires the same participants is carried over for several years.

For instance, in the case of the Mid-Atlantic dialogue, the subject of interreligious marriage between Muslims and Catholics was rather exhaustively examined. The effort produced a document, titled *Marriage: Roman Catholic and Sunni Muslim Perspectives*, which sets forth, in both a descriptive and a pastoral way, the considerably different understandings of marriage in the two religions. To its credit, *Marriage* provides a good deal of sober advice in presenting the very substantial religious and cultural differences that any Catholic-Muslim marriage would have to overcome (which occurs only in the case of a Catholic woman marrying a Muslim man, as Muslim women are forbidden from marrying Catholic men). While it refers to the different status of men and women in Islam, it does not deal with the issue of polygamy, the statutory inferiority of women in shari'a, or of the Qur'anically sanctioned use of violence against a disobedient wife. Perhaps this is because of the illegality of polygamy and domestic violence in the United States, along with the legal inapplicability of shari'a, or possibly out of a desire not to offend – though this omission might leave the Catholic wife of a Muslim husband, who returned with him to a Muslim country in which polygamy is legal, in a most unfortunate situation. However, in general, this document is a good example of what dialogue can produce that is of practical pastoral use, and it soundly discourages such marriages with persuasive reasons from both sides.

It is also unusual in respect to its utility. Many of the other dialogue exchanges seem to have been held at the level of primers on the respective religions: Catholics teaching Muslims about Christianity, and Muslims teaching Catholics about Islam. For instance, sessions have been held on the respective understandings of "the Word of God," "Stories of Abraham," "the Story of Joseph," "Migration in the Lives of Jesus, Mohammed," and the miraculous story of the "seven sleepers of Ephesus," as found in early Christian writings and in Surah 18 of the Qur'an.

This, of course, can be useful, so long as there are no misrepresentations or misunderstandings. Here, however, a problem arises. Islam is not homogeneous. Unlike Catholicism, it has no papacy that can enunciate universally agreed-upon doctrine. It has orthopraxis, rather than orthodoxy. Therefore, the danger exists that the resulting representation of what "we" Catholics and Muslims have agreed upon might not extend much beyond the people in the room. Within Islam, the most aggravated differences exist between the majority Sunnis and the minority Shi'as, but there are also very substantial differences among Sunnis between, for example, Islamists and more mainstream adherents to the faith. Among the Sunnis, the Islamists tend to be the activists and they, therefore, often dominate in the organizations purporting to represent Islam as a whole.

Also, without a deep knowledge of Islam, it can be difficult to decode exactly what is being said by some of the Muslim participants. For example, in 2003, the West Coast dialogue issued a lengthy statement, "Friends and Not

Adversaries: a Catholic-Muslim Spiritual Journey," which reports on four years of dialogue meetings. A good deal of what is in this document is well-meaning and anodyne, but substantial parts of it can be at the same time very misleading. As is the case in all three regional conferences, whenever the issue of religious freedom is raised, there is never a mention of the absence of freedom of conscience in all four Sunni legal schools or of the death penalty for apostasy that is likewise prescribed. Instead, the "Friends" document states that "we are aware that this ideal has not been fully realized at all times by every religious group and that this prescribed religious pluralism has not been characteristic of every historical era. The advancement of religious freedom is a long-term undertaking..." Indeed, it is, especially in some Muslim countries, where it does not exist. Failure to mention this and the reasons for it may be polite in dialogue, but misleading in substance. There are frequent references to the troubles Muslims suffer in the United States as victims of negative "stereotyping," but there is not one reference in the conference summaries or press releases to the widespread persecution of Christians in Muslim-majority countries. Why have there been no joint statements condemning persecution of Copts in Egypt, for instance? Perhaps because the reaction would have been the same as it was at Al-Azhar University, which broke off dialogue with the Vatican after Benedict XVI expressed his concern (see footnote 1).

When the Midwest Muslim Catholic Dialogue undertook to explore "In the Public Square: Catholics and Muslims on Religious Freedom," it did so only within the American context. In other words, it was examining whether the United States was complying with religious freedom. The summary of the conference, issued by the USCCB, states that "both Catholic and Islamic notions of law and the human person presuppose a set of basic rights conferred by the Creator. From their theological perspectives, Muslims and Catholics will tend to support the notion of 'inalienable rights.'"

The supposition of a common set of basic rights grounded in theology is entirely wrong. As stated earlier, the notion of "inalienable rights" is not familiar to Islam, which acknowledges only God-given duties, not rights, in its theology. Inalienable rights would have to be inherent in humanity, a product of natural law, which mainstream Sunni Islam denies. We have already examined what the *Cairo Declaration of Human Rights* means in this respect: shari'a.

Likewise, it is highly problematic for the participants to announce that they "fundamentally agree on the nature of peace and justice" without explicitly defining these terms. One of the Muslim imams stated in his presentation that "it is God who explains justice and expects righteous behavior. Quran 12:40 makes this point: Sovereignty belongs to God, and humanity serves God by being righteous and implementing justice and not by pretending to make or to abrogate divine law."

A Christian might be ready to agree with this statement without understanding what is actually being said by the Muslim imam. A number of standard Islamic themes are being referred to here. First of all, Surah 40 states that "Legislation is not but for Allah." This is in accord with the teaching that humans do not exercise sovereignty, but only God does. Therefore, humans have no authority to make laws. This has been referred to earlier in the principle of Islamic jurisprudence that "reason is not a legislator."

As we have also seen, in mainstream Sunni theology, reason is considered incapable of apprehending what is just because *nothing is just or unjust in itself*, but only as God says so. Therefore, what is just can be known only through God's revelation, which is the Qur'an and the Sunnah – not through reason. Did the Catholic participants, who included an archbishop, understand that they had just agreed to "the nature of justice" being a form of Islamic divine positivism, or that, in doing so, they had abandoned the natural law teachings on justice from Augustine and Aquinas and other doctors of the church? Most certainly, they did not, because they did not understand the meaning of what was being said in its Islamic context.

This is likewise the case in the common affirmations concerning the nature of peace. The meaning of peace is undefined, except for the necessity of justice as its foundation. Both Muslim and Catholic participants agree on the essential connection between peace and justice but, as we have just seen, justice can mean something quite different to a Muslim. So too can peace. The goal of Islam is *salam*, which means "peace" in Arabic. However, ultimate peace is achieved only by bringing all things into submission to Islam. How is that to be done? That submission is signified by the rule of shari'a.

Does this mean that all American Muslims are exponents of a shari'a state and are attempting to install one here? No, it does not mean this. In fact, many Muslim immigrants come to the United States precisely to avoid such a situation, and the majority of them are happily assimilated here. However, the pull of this part of Islam is nonetheless felt particularly from the Muslim organizations that claim to represent them. Dr. Muzammil Siddiqi, a frequent dialogue partner and past president of the Islamic Society of North America (ISNA), had this to say in an October 18, 1996 issue of the newspaper *Pakistan Link*: "We must not forget that Allah's rules have to be established in all lands, and all our efforts should lead to that direction." In 2001, he wrote, "Once more people accept Islam, insha'allah, this will lead to the implementation of Sharia in all areas."

A small example can be telling of the way in which this principle operates incrementally, particularly since it involved one of the prominent members of the West Coast Dialogue. In 1997, a group of Muslim organizations, including the Council on American Islamic Relations (CAIR), objected to the carved stone depiction of Muhammad in the U.S. Supreme Court's pantheon of 18 prominent lawgivers of history. Muhammad is portrayed holding a Qur'an in one hand and a sword in the other. Though there are exceptions in Ottoman and Persian history, the general rule in Islam is not to portray Muhammad's face in any art form. There were also objections to the presence of the sword as giving a false image of a bellicose Islam. In the *Minaret* newspaper, which he edits, Dr. Aslam Abdullah, a soon-to-be West Coast dialogue participant, suggested that an appropriate response by the Supreme Court would be "to remove the picture with the sword and the Quran and replace it with a Quranic verse emphasizing law and justice." He added, "Muslim scholars say the Prophet himself commanded his companions not to carve his pictures." Acceding to this request would, of course, have brought the Supreme Court into compliance with Islamic law, which is, however, irrelevant to the "laws of Nature and of Nature's God" on which the authority of the Court is based.

Other misunderstandings arise from the very different contexts in which the same things are said. However, some statements verge on misrepresentation and dissimulation. One hesitates to say this, because the views expressed may be sincerely held by the specific Muslim participants but, then again, they may not.[7] The point is that these views, in certain cases, do not necessarily represent Islam. Consider, for instance, the statement from Dr. Muzammil Siddiqi in a 2001 West Coast Dialogue that "aggression is never allowed in matters of faith" in Islam.[8] In the way in which this statement was most probably understood

---

[7] One must keep in mind that religious dissimulation or deception (*taqiyya*) is sanctioned in Islam if Muslims believe they are in dangerously hostile circumstances or, sometimes, if lying is necessary to advance the cause of Islam. See: http://www.meforum.org/2538/taqiyya-islam-rules-of-war

[8] This is a reference to the verse (Q 2:256) "There is no compulsion (*ikraha*) in religion." However, this is not the main theme of the Qur'an and the *hadith*, where the option of "Islam or the sword" and the statement that "the Religion of Muhammad was spread by the sword" are ubiquitous. Compulsion was applied in different degrees in different circumstances; in the Arabian Peninsula, no "polytheists" could remain; they had to accept "Islam or the sword." Jews were expelled from the Arabian Peninsula (and are formally barred from it even today by the Saudi regime) and, in other areas that fell under Muslim sway, Jews and Christians had to accept the "Pact of Omar" that defined their status as second-class inhabitants. While Jews, Christians, and Zoroastrians were not exactly "compelled" to accept Islam formally, the pressure of discrimination was intended to bring about such a result, and did.

by the Catholic participants, one could only wish that it were true, but it decidedly is not, except in the most literal way in which shari'a defines as aggressors those who refuse to accept Islam. In classical Islamic jurisprudence, after Islam has been offered to non-Muslim states or entities three times, their refusal to accept it makes them the aggressor. Anything that inhibits the spread of Islam is considered a hostile act insofar as it contradicts the will of Allah that "the word of Allah be supreme in the world," and is hence a *casus belli*. Waging this kind of offensive jihad (*jihad al-talab waal-ibtida*) was an *obligation* of the caliph or "commander of the faithful" at least once a year, conditions permitting. Muslims did not use the word *harb* (generic war) to describe their consequent armed assaults, but *jihad*, and considered them "openings" (*futuhat*) of the world to Islam. It is those who resist Islam who are waging *harb*. Therefore, Dr. Siddiqui, who earned a graduate degree in Arabic and Islamic Studies at the Islamic University of Medina in Saudi Arabia, is literally correct in his statements that "aggression is never allowed," but only through the legerdemain of shari'a, which defines defense against Islam as aggression.[9] How many of his Catholic interlocutors might have understood this distinction? Apparently, none.

In a 2004 Midwest Regional Dialogue, there is another example that borders on misrepresentation. According to the USCCB press release, "the participants found that our respective traditions have been intellectually nurtured by the Hellenistic philosophical tradition in the field of ethics, in a description of the virtues, and in our ways of articulating excellence in a meaningful human life. The texts of our respective scriptural revelations, Biblical and Quranic, complete in divine terms what reason begins in its human quest for perfection." The fantastical level of equivalence suggested in these two sentences is extraordinary. Obviously, none of the participants raised the subject of the de-hellenization of Islam from the *Regensburg Lecture*[10] or of Sunni Islam's explicit denial of the ability to apprehend morality through reason. There is no need to repeat the history, briefly stated earlier, of how thoroughly Sunni Islam turned its back on its heritage of Greek philosophy or on any notion of natural law that would define what human perfection is. Its having done so constitutes the main problems

---

[9] One is reminded of the advice given by Ahmad ibn Naqib al-Misri in *Reliance of the Traveller* concerning permissible lying: "But it is religiously more precautionary in all such cases to employ words that give a misleading impression, meaning to intend by one's words something that is literally true, in respect to which one is not lying, while the outward purport of the words

[10] In fact, in the USCCB press releases summarizing 30 Catholic-Muslim dialogues from its regional conferences, the *Regensburg Lecture* is mentioned only once, in the 2007 Midwest meeting.

we are facing today from the highly dysfunctional Muslim Arab world.[11] Any Catholic participant who agreed to the quotation above would have to have been completely ignorant of these things. Whether done through ignorance or goodwill, the fostering of this misrepresentation is an example of the substantial harm that misguided dialogue can do. How can we know the defining differences if they are denied, and their opposites are asserted in their place?

This also raises the question of the validity and suitability of the Muslim organizations that the regional bishops' conferences have chosen as their counterparts. The heterogeneity of Islam makes it difficult to ascertain who might be the most appropriate partners in dialogue, and the easiest thing to do is to choose the most visible Muslim organizations that claim the largest representation. This is apparently what the USCCB has done. The most frequent partners are the Islamic Society of North America (ISNA), the Islamic Circle of North America, and the Islamic Shura Council of California, in cooperation with ISNA. There is also sometimes participation from members of the Council on American Islamic Relations (CAIR).

There are problems with most of these groups, as outlined by Hedieh Mirahmadi, President of the World Organization for Resource Development and Education and a contributor to a book titled *The Other Muslims: Moderate and Secular*. She writes, "Thanks to their relentless activism, over time Islamists took control of many existing mosques and Muslim charities, and (again with the help of petrodollars) built hundreds of new mosques, religious schools, and community centers across the United States. Using tactics similar to the communists they organized domestic organizations to speak for American Muslims, making sure that their voice was the only one heard."

Mirahmadi argues that "While the Islamists are successful in taking over leadership of many Islamic organizations and institutions, their views do not represent the vast majority of moderate, mainstream American Muslims."

Husain Haqqani, scholar and former Pakistan Ambassador to the United States, described the result: "The mosques and organizations [in the U.S.] all ended up, or most of them ended up under Muslim Brotherhood control." In a 2008 report on "The Muslim Brotherhood's U.S. Network," Muslim scholar Zeyno Baran of the Hudson Institute supported this claim, saying, "Most prominent Muslim organizations in America were either created by, or are as-

---

[11] Anyone who considers this an exaggeration should read the *UN Arab Human Development Reports*, written by Arabs, who catalog the miserable conditions in the Middle East as the worst in the world in every category of human development, except for sub-Saharan Africa.

sociated with, the Muslim Brotherhood and have therefore been heavily influenced by Islamist ideology."[12]

Yet it is with these Islamists that the bishops' regional conferences mainly speak. Clearly, there has been insufficient scrutiny of dialogue partners. What, one may ask, is the problem with the Muslim Brotherhood, and why would an association with it, or with its allies, present a difficulty for the bishops' conferences? The Brotherhood, or *Ikhwan*, is increasingly well known from its recent successes throughout the Middle East in the wake of the Arab Spring. Founded in 1928 by Hassan al-Banna, the Brotherhood aims for the rule of shari'a and the resuscitation of the caliphate. It is the quintessential Islamist organization, and has spawned many allied groups, such as Hamas. But few Americans have been aware of the Brotherhood's intentions and activities in the United States. Only with the Holy Land Foundation Terrorism Funding Trial in 2008 has awareness increased. The trial established that a majority of the large Muslim organizations in the U.S. are, or were, linked to the Muslim Brotherhood and Hamas, its Palestinian branch.

Most importantly, the trial evidence disclosed a strategy memo, written by Mohamad Akram, AKA Adlouni, dated May 22, 1991, that spells out the role of the Muslim Brotherhood in North America and includes a list of all Muslim Brotherhood organizations "and the organizations of our friends" in North America as of that time.

The strategy memo declares that "The process of settlement is a 'Civilization-Jihadist Process' with all the word means. The Ikhwan [Brotherhood] must understand that their work in America is a kind of grand Jihad in eliminating and destroying the Western civilization from within and 'sabotaging' its miserable house by their hands and the hands of the believers so that it is eliminated and God's religion is made victorious over all other religions" (*U.S. v. Holy Land Foundation* [TXND 3:04cr240] Government Exhibit 003-0085; "An Explanatory Memorandum on the General Strategic Goal for the Group in North America").

---

[12] "Marcia Hermansen of Loyola University in Chicago has written that followers of Barelvism – the majority trend among Muslims in the Indian subcontinent and the South Asian Sunni communities abroad – have given up organizing a body to represent their interests in America. Barelvis are traditionalists opposed to Deobandism, and who support instead Sufi spirituality and who proclaim loyalty to non-Muslim authorities. According to Hermansen, their 'failure may have occurred as a result of factors specific to the Muslim subculture in the United States, for example, the fact that most community organizations were already controlled by anti-Sufi Islamists' – an assessment that is unfortunately accurate." – Irfan Al-Alawi, Gatestone Institute.

The Islamic Society of North America (ISNA) was first on the list of organizations in the strategy memo, which also included the Muslim Students Association (MSA), the Muslim American Society (MAS), the Islamic Circle of North America (ICNA), and the ISNA Fiqh Committee, or what is now the Fiqh Council of North America. In the trial, ISNA was named among "individuals/entities who are and/or were members of the US Muslim Brotherhood." ISNA, NAIT, CAIR and several related organizations were listed as unindicted co-conspirators. When CAIR and ISNA attempted to have their names removed as an unindicted co-conspirators, United States District Judge Jorge Solis refused, with the following, revealing explanation:

> Finally, CAIR, NAIT and ISNA asked the Court to strike their names from any public document filed or issued by the government. (Mot. At 6.) While it is clear from the *Briggs* line of cases that the Government should have originally filed the unindicted co-conspirators' names under seal, the court declines to strike CAIR, ISNA and NAIT's names from those documents. The Government has produced ample evidence to establish the associations of CAIR, ISNA and NAIT with HLF, the Islamic Association for Palestine ("IAP"), and with Hamas. While the Court recognizes that the evidence produced by the government largely predates the HLF designation date, the evidence is nonetheless sufficient to show the association of these entities with HLF, IAP, and Hamas... Thus, maintaining the names of the entities on the list is appropriate in light of the evidence proffered by the Government. (July 1, 2009)

Alongside the court's decision, it is also significant that Congress, in H.R. 2112 (signed into law on November 18, 2011), expressed its support of the FBI policy prohibiting any formal cooperation with unindicted co-conspirators in terrorism cases, unless related to an investigation.

One also ought to be aware of the Brotherhood view of interfaith dialogue as expressed by Sayyid Qutb (executed by Nasser in 1966), the principal formulator of the Brotherhood ideology, whose writings are perhaps the single most powerful source behind the Islamist movement today. Because of their significance, they are worth quoting at length (from his book, *Milestones*):

> They call for "co-existence" ... for the "coming together of faiths", for "inter-faith dialogue." Not in order that Truth should be distinguished from Evil and thereby followed ... but for the co-existence of

Truth *alongside* Evil within one garment, so that principles, concepts and values become mingled with each other … so that the conflict between Truth and Evil be removed, [a conflict] that is ancient, and dates from when God Almighty created Adam and Iblis, and which shall continue to the Day of Resurrection!

The effect of this sinful call is that it erases the differences between Islam and disbelief, between truth and falsehood, good and bad, and it breaks the wall of resentment between the Muslims and the unbelievers, so that there is no more loyalty and enmity, no more jihad and fighting to raise Allah's word on earth.

The chasm between Islam and Jahiliyyah [pre-Muhammadan ignorance and polytheism] is great, and a bridge is not to be built across it so that the people on the two sides may mix with each other, but *only so that the people of Jahiliyyah may come over to Islam*" (my emphasis).

There could not be a clearer statement that the original Brotherhood's principal objective in interfaith dialogue was to proselytize, not to understand or befriend.

Similar problems exist with the Islamic Circle of North America (ICNA), which was founded in 1971 as an American affiliate of *Jamaat-e-Islami* (JI), a major Islamist organization in Pakistan that helped to establish the Taliban. The organization utilizes materials from Islamists such as JI founder Syed Abul A'la Maududi, who, along with al-Banna and Qutb, was a principal formulator of the Islamist ideology.

These groups may or may not have maintained their links to the Muslim Brotherhood, but their lineage should at least give the USCCB pause in regards to its open association with them. If the FBI prohibits formal cooperation with unindicted co-conspirators, perhaps the USCCB should also. Taking these organizations as public partners in dialogue further legitimizes them, strengthens the impression that they are the true voice of Islam in the United States, and reinforces their attempted monopolization of Islam in America. The Muslims capable of real dialogue are marginalized.

One American Muslim who objects to this is Dr. Zuhdi Jasser, founder of the American Islamic Forum for Democracy, who said, "Most interesting is this position of the Catholic Church [USCCB] in the U.S. because of how out of step it seems with Pope Benedict's understanding of the challenges Muslims have in confronting societies based in reason as articulated, for example, in his Regensburg speech. While as a devout Muslim I may not agree with all of Pope Benedict's points in that lecture, the essence of the conflict between Islamism

and reason is very important and one entirely ignored by this unfortunate relationship between Catholic leadership and ISNA." Jasser warned that "They
are simply reaching for the lowest hanging fruit to represent Muslims. They are
ignoring their ideologies and trusting their superficial condemnations of terrorism and the ideologies that feed it. I dissect ISNA in my book and my own
experiences with their conventions and leaders, like when I saw Imam Siraj
Wahhaj call for the replacement of the U.S. Constitution with the Quran in his
keynote address to their annual convention of 1995."[13]

Allying with these groups may also produce some strange fruit. Consider
the remarks of Cardinal Theodore McCarrick, the Catholic archbishop emeritus
of Washington, D.C., at the National Press Club during a press conference, September 8, 2010, sponsored by the Islamic Society of North America (ISNA), in
support of the Ground Zero mosque and to denounce anti-Muslim bigotry. Mc-
Carrick, a featured speaker, said, "I think it was because I have been very much
involved with the [Ground Zero mosque issue] – with a good Muslim leadership here – in this part of the country, especially with the – with the addition of
the Islamic Society of North America." At the same event, he told
CNSNews.com that if "someone sees the Gospel as the truth of God's presence
in our world, that person should embrace the Gospel." He also said, however,
"If a person sees the Quran as proof of God's presence in the world, then I cannot say, 'Don't embrace the Quran.'" Qutb would have been pleased with the
double endorsement of ISNA and the Qur'an by a Catholic cardinal. These are
the fruits of dialogue at which Islamists aim: the utilization of the Church for
purposes of Islamic *dawa*.

As Dr. Sandra Toenies Keating said, "In the end, we may not be able to overcome the impasse, but it is critical to know where it lies. Knowing where our
difference lies has enormous implications for how one regards the way in which
to proceed in contemporary relations, dialogue, and the goals of evangelization
and mission, preaching and teaching, even the theological enterprise." Indeed
it does and, in this respect, much of the Catholic-Muslim dialogue conducted
through the USCCB seems to have not met this standard. It has obscured, indeed obfuscated, the location and nature of the difference: not in terms of
Catholic doctrine, which it has consistently upheld, but in failing to discern and
insist upon what Islam in the main really teaches. In this respect, it is perhaps
more deceived than deceiving. Regardless, the results are confusing and there-

---

13 http://www.wnd.com/2013/02/moderate-muslim-calls-for-battle-with-jihadists
   /#2OW2hHyZqtkEBbHo.99

fore harmful. Recall Benedict XVI's remark that "truth makes consensus possible." Consensus not based on truth will be false, and possibly injurious.

Catholic-Muslim dialogue in the United States requires a major reevaluation in terms of the organizations involved, the personnel participating (see addendum), and the substance addressed. It should have chosen, and could now choose, different Muslim interlocutors who themselves genuinely wish for a rehellenization of their culture and faith, so that real dialogue can be held on how to achieve this and other important things.

The single most surprising, and disappointing, thing about the 30 dialogue conferences for which information is publicly available is that the need for a rehellenization of Islam is never addressed in a major, serious way. Yet it is upon this that the future of real dialogue depends. The year before becoming pope, Cardinal Joseph Ratzinger said that "without peace between reason and faith, there cannot be peace at the world level, because without peace between reason and religion, the very sources of morals and the rule of law dry out." As contentious as the *Regensburg Lecture* may have seemed to many in the Muslim world and elsewhere, it was necessary. Islam needs peace within itself in the very way in which Ratzinger spoke, between reason and faith. The lack of that peace is at the source of the strife in the Muslim world today. Islam is at war with itself. To pretend otherwise does a disservice to Muslims and Christians alike. Of course, if reason is reduced to a "Western concept," this peace will never happen, which is why reason's integrity must be insisted on by both sides in the dialogue. Benedict XVI has been perhaps the greatest defender of reason in the West, if not the world, in recent years. The Catholic side is ready for this conversation. So are a number of Muslims who share the same diagnosis of the ills of our time. With them, one can have a very real "Common Word." Whether or not there can be "peace at the world level" may very well depend on their influence prevailing within their own faith. As difficult as that might be, should not dialogue aim to help this happen?

Addendum:
Muslim Participants in
US Catholic Dialogue, 2000-2011

(By year, from the most recent back to 2000,
with repetitions included to indicate frequency of attendance)

Mid Atlantic Catholic Muslim dialogue:

Ataullah Siddiqi, Ph.D., fellow at Woodstock Theological Center at Georgetown University; ICNA president Zahid Bukhari, Ph.D.; Imam Hamad Ahmad Chebli, Islamic Society of Central New Jersey; Imam Hafiz Zafeer Ali, ICNA Headquarters; Imam Muhammad Abdul Jabban, Ph.D., Masjid Darul Qur'an, Bayshore, New York; Shaykh Abdool Rahman Khan, Resident Scholar, Islamic Foundation Villa Park, Chicago; Muhhammad T. Rahman, secretary general, ICNA, Jamaica, New York; and Naeem Baig, Ph.D., vice president, ICNA, dialogue staff.

Dr. Talat Sultan of the Islamic Circle of North America (ICNA); ICNA President Dr. Zahid Bukhari; Imam Hamad Ahmad Chebli, Islamic Society of Central New Jersey; Dr. Safaa Zarzour, President of the Islamic Society of North America; Shaykh Abdur Rahman Khan, Resident Scholar, Islamic Foundation Villa Park, Chicago; Imam Zafeer Ali Hafiz, ICNA Headquarters; Dr. Naeem Baig, Vice President, ICNA; Moein Khawaja, Council on American-Islamic Relations; and Imam Sohaib Sultan, Muslim Chaplain, Princeton University.

Imam Ahmed Nezar Kobeisy; Zahid Bukhari, Ph.D., newly-elected President of ICNA; and Imam Kobeisy, who assisted as Muslim co-chair. Other participants included Shabbir Mansuri of the Institute on Religion and Civic Values and Imam Zafeer Ali Hafiz from ICNA headquarters.

Shabbir Mansuri; Munir Shaikh; Safaa Zarzour; Ameer Khurshid Khan, President of ICNA; Imam Dr. Ahmed Nezar Kobeisy; Imam Hamad Ahmad Chebli; Shabbir Mansuri; Munir Shaikh; Safaa Zarzour; Prof. Zahid Bukhari; Radouan Majidi.

Dr. Safaa Zarzour of the Council of Greater Chicago Muslim Organizations; Mohammad Tariq Sherwani, Director, Muslim Center of New York; M. Shamsheer Ali Baig, ICNA; Azeem Khan, ICNA; Imam Shamsi Ali, Jamaica Muslim Center/Islamic Cultural Center of New York; Imam Hamad Ahmad Chebli, Islamic Society of Central New Jersey; Rafeek Mohamed, principal of Al-Ihsan Academy, Imam of Masjid Al-Ikhlas; Dr. Safaa Zarzour, Council of Greater Chicago Muslim Organizations; Imam Safee Ali, ICNA.

Dr. Younas Shahid; Imam Mohamed el Filali; Prof. Esmet Kamil; Imam Ashraf uz Zaman Khan; Mr. Mohammad T. Sherwani; Susan Georgini; Manzar Karim; Hamad A. Chebli; Azeem Khan.

Dr. Khurshid Khan of the Central Majlis As-Sura in Jamaica, NY; Muhammad T. Rahman; Younas Shahid; Dr. Esmet Kamil; Imam Ibrahim Negm; Dr. Khurshid Khan; Imam Mohamed el Filali; Imam Hamad Ahmad Chebli; Nashar Khan.

Dr. Ibrahim Negm, Islamic Center of South Shore; Dr. Khurshid Khan, representing ICNA; Mr. Salman Yusuff, New Jersey State Prison Chaplaincy; Naim Baig, ICNA Secretary General; Muhammad Tariq Rahman, ICNA Relief; Dr. Esmet Kamil, Pratt Institute.

Dr. Khurshid Khan, ICNA; Mr. Salman Yusuff, Philadelphia; Mr. Muhammad Tariq Rahman, ICNA; Mr. Mohamed el Filali, Newark; Imam Hamad Ahmad Chebli, Monmouth Junction; Mr. Tariq Shahid, New York; Dr. Viqar Hamdani, New York; Mr. John Abdul-Malek Ellis, New York.

Dr. Khurshid Khan, representing ICNA; Sheikh Ibrahim Nejm, Valley Stream, Long Island; Dr. Khalid Qazi; Dr. Zahid Bukhari, Georgetown University; Dr. Salman Yusuf, Vineland, New Jersey; Imam Hamad Ahmad Chebli, Islamic Society of Central New Jersey; Imam Salihou Djabi, Masjid Malcolm Shabazz, Harlem, New York; Al-Haaj Ghazi Khankan, Islamic Center of Long Island.

Dr. Khalid Qazi, Buffalo; Mr. Salman Yusuf, Philadelphia; Mr. Ali Dataee, Islamic Society of Greater Harrisburg; Al-Haaj Ghazi Khankan, Islamic Center of Long Island; Sheikh Ibrahim Najm; Dr. Zahid Bukhari, ICNA Director for Interreligious Relations.

Midwest Catholic Muslim dialogue:

Dr. Sayyid Syeed; Dr. Ghulam-Haider Aasi, American Islamic College; Mr. Victor Begg, Council of Islamic Organizations of Michigan; Ms. Insharah Farhoud, Islamic Society of Milwaukee; Dr. Irfan Omar, Professor of Islamic Studies, Marquette University; Dr. Zeki Saritoprak; Dr. Zufilqar Ali Shah, Islamic Center of Milwaukee; Dr. Sayyid Syeed.

Dr. Sayyid M. Syeed, Islamic Society of North America; Dr. Ghulam-Haider Aasi, Professor, American Islamic College; Inshirah Farhoud, Outreach Coordinator, Islamic Society of Milwaukee; Mohammad O. Farooq, Associate Professor of Economics & Finance, Upper Iowa University; Dr. Irfan Omar; Dr. Saritoprak; Dr. Zulfiqar Ali Shah.

Shayk Mongy El-Quesny of the Islamic Center; Mohamed Elsanousi, Director of Communications and Community Outreach of the Islamic Society of North America; Dr. Sayyid M. Syeed, ISNA; Shayk Mongy El-Quesny, Northwest Indiana Islamic Center; Â Mohammed Elsanousi, National Office, ISNA; Inshirah Farhoud, Islamic Society of Milwaukee; Dr. Gulam Haider Aasi, American Islamic College, Chicago, Illinois.

Sayyid M. Syeed, Ph.D., ISNA; Imam Hassan al-Qazwini, Islamic Center of America; Inshirah Farhoud, Islamic Society of Milwaukee; Eide Alawan, Islamic Center of America; Victor Ghalib Begg, Council of Islamic Organizations of Michigan; Mohammad Omar Farooq, Ph.D., Upper Iowa University; Dr. Shahid Athar, Interfaith Alliance of Indianapolis; Gulam Haider Aasi, Ph.D., American Islamic College, Chicago, Illinois.

Dr. Sayyid M. Syeed, ISNA; Dr. Muhammad Shafiq, Center for Interfaith Studies and Dialogue, Rochester, NY; Imam Hassan al-Qazwini; Dr. Anas Malik, Xavier University; Intisar Khanani; Michael Saahir, Nur-Allah Islamic Center; Inshirah Farhoud, Islamic Society of Milwaukee; Eide Alawan, Islamic Center of America; Victor Ghalib Begg, Council of Islamic Organizations of Michigan; Muktar Ahmad, Islamic Society of North America; Ashfaq Lodhi, Islamic Society of North America; Dr. Khalid Mahmoud.

Dr. Sayyid M. Syeed, ISNA; Dr. Muhammad Shafiq, Center for Interfaith Studies and Dialogue, Rochester, NY; Louay Safi, ISNA; Dr. Anas Malik, Xavier University; Michael Saahir, Nur-Allah Islamic Center; Dr. Ghouse A. Shareef, Islamic Cultural Center; Inshirah Farhoud, Islamic Society of Milwaukee.

Dr. Sayyid M. Syeed; Dr. Shahid Athar; Dr. Ghouse A. Shareef; Mrs. Sameena D. Shareef; Sheikh Muhammad Nur Abdullah; Dr. Ghulam-Haider Aasi; Naheed Arshad; Mr. Muktar Ahmad; Dr. Muhammad Shafiq; Dr. Aras Malik; Dr. Iqbal Malik.

Imam Mohammad Ali Elahi; Dr. Irfan Ahmad Khan, Council of Islamic Organizations, Chicago; Dr. Ghulam Haider Aasi, American Islamic College; Imam Muhammad Nur Abdullah, Dar-ul-Salam Masjid, St. Louis; Dr. M. Iqbal Malik, Carmel, Indiana; Dr. Ghouse A. Shareef, Louisville; Imam Fawaz Damra, Cleveland; Dr. Shahid Athar, Indianapolis.

West Coast Catholic Muslim dialogue:

Dr. Muzammil Siddiqi, Islamic Society of Orange County; Sherrel Johnson, Council on American-Islamic Relations (CAIR) – California; Imam Taha Hassane, Islamic Center of San Diego; Mr. Hussam Ayloush, CAIR – Greater Los Angeles Area; Saideh Khan and Jerrel Abdul Salaam, active members of the local Muslim community.

Dr. Muzammil Siddiqi; Imam Sayed Mostafa Qazwini; Sherrel Johnson; Jerrel Abdul Salaam; Dr. Iftekhar A. Hai; Dr. Hussam Ayloush; Imam Taha Hassane.

Dr. Muzammil Siddiqi; Imam Sayed Mostafa Qazwini; Hussam Ayloush; Imam Taha Hassane; Kalim Farooki; Sherrel Johnson; Saideh Khan; Dr. Hussam Ayloush.

Muzammil H. Siddiqi, Director, Islamic Society of Orange County; Imam Sayed Moustafa al-Qazwini, Director, Islamic Educational Center of Orange County; Iftekhar Hai, United Muslims of America; Dr. Karim T. Abdullah; Imam Sadiq Safir; Mrs. Saide Khan; Mrs. Sherrel Johnson, CAIR; Kalim Farooki, Shura Council of Southern California; Dr. Maryam Kim Kieu, M.D., M.P.H.; Hussam Ayloush, Executive Director, CAIR Los Angeles; Imam Taha Hassane, Islamic Center of San Diego; Khalil Momand, Islamic Center of South Bay, Los Angeles.

Dr. Muzamil Siddiqi; Sadeh Khan; Mustafa al-Qaswini; Karim Abdullah; Maryam Kimquy Kieu; Jerrel Abdul Salaam; Fatima Saleh; Sherrel Johnson; Samina F. Sundas; Shakeel Shad; Muzamil Siddiqi; Yasi Fazaga.

Dr. Muzammil H. Siddiqi, Islamic Society of Orange County; Karim Abdullah; Sherell A. Johnson; Mostafa Al-Qazwini.

Dr. Muzammil Siddiqi, Director, Islamic Society of Orange County; Imam Mustafa Al-Qazwini, Director, Islamic Education Center of Orange County; Dr. Aslam Abdullah; Imam Sadiq Saafir; Mr. Naim Shah Jr., Los Angeles; Mrs. Saideh Khan, Costa Mesa; Jerrel Abdul Salaam, Paramount, California; Fatima Saleh, Costa Mesa; Sherrel A. Johnson, Council of American-Islamic Relations, California.

Dr. Muzammil H. Siddiqi, Director, Islamic Society of Orange County; Dr. Ahmad Sakr, Foundation for Islamic Knowledge; Kalim Farooki, Corona, California; Imam Abuqadir Al-Amin, San Francisco, California; Imam Sabir El-Amin, Los Angeles, California; Jerrel Abdul Salam, Paramount, California; Dr. Aslam Abdullah, Los Angeles, California; Salam al-Marayati, Los Angeles, California; Imam Sadiq Saafir, Pasadena, California; Naim Shah, Jr.

About the Author

Robert Reilly is a senior fellow at the American Foreign Policy Council and a member of the board of the Westminster Institute and of the Middle East Media Research Institute. He has taught at the National Defense University and served in the Office of The Secretary of Defense, where he was Senior Advisor for Information Strategy (2002-2006). He participated in Operation Iraqi Freedom in 2003, as Senior Advisor to the Iraqi Ministry of Information. Before that, he was director of the Voice of America, where he had worked the prior decade. Mr. Reilly has served in the White House as a Special Assistant to the President (1983-1985), and in the U.S. Information Agency both in D.C. and abroad. In the private sector, he spent more than seven years with the Intercollegiate Studies Institute, as both national director and then president. He attended Georgetown University and the Claremont Graduate University. He has published widely on foreign policy, "war of ideas" issues, Islam, and classical music. His book, *The Closing of the Muslim Mind: How Intellectual Suicide Created the Modern Islamist Crisis*, was published by ISI Press. His recent monograph, *Islam and the West: The Theology behind the History*, was published by CRCE in London.

About the Publishers

The Westminster Institute is a non-profit organization based in McLean, Virginia, whose mission is to promote individual dignity and freedom for people throughout the world. The Institute fulfills this mission by sponsoring high-quality independent research by scholars and policy analysts, with a particular focus on the threats posed by extremism and radical ideologies. The Institute is supported by contributions from individuals and private foundations.

The **Faith & Reason Institute** is a think-tank based in Washington, D.C., that works to recover the ancient Western understanding of human knowledge and divine revelation as co-ordinate calls upon the human spirit that need to be translated into everyday practice. The Institute addresses questions of economics, politics, public policy, science, technology, the environment and public culture from the perspective of both faith and reason. It does so by conducting research, conferences, seminars, and publishing.